CONFESSIONS OF A CRAZED TOUR GUIDE

CONFESSIONS OF A CRAZED TOUR GUIDE

June Harvey

gatekeeper press
Tampa, Florida

The content associated with this book is the sole work and responsibility of the author. Gatekeeper Press had no involvement in the generation of this content.

Confessions of a Crazed Tour Guide

Published by Gatekeeper Press
7853 Gunn Hwy., Suite 209
Tampa, FL 33626
www.GatekeeperPress.com

Copyright © 2024 by June Harvey

All rights reserved. Neither this book, nor any parts within it may be sold or reproduced in any form or by any electronic or mechanical means, including information storage and retrieval systems, without permission in writing from the author. The only exception is by a reviewer, who may quote short excerpts in a review.

Library of Congress Control Number: 2023951510

ISBN (paperback): 9781662946165
eISBN: 9781662946172

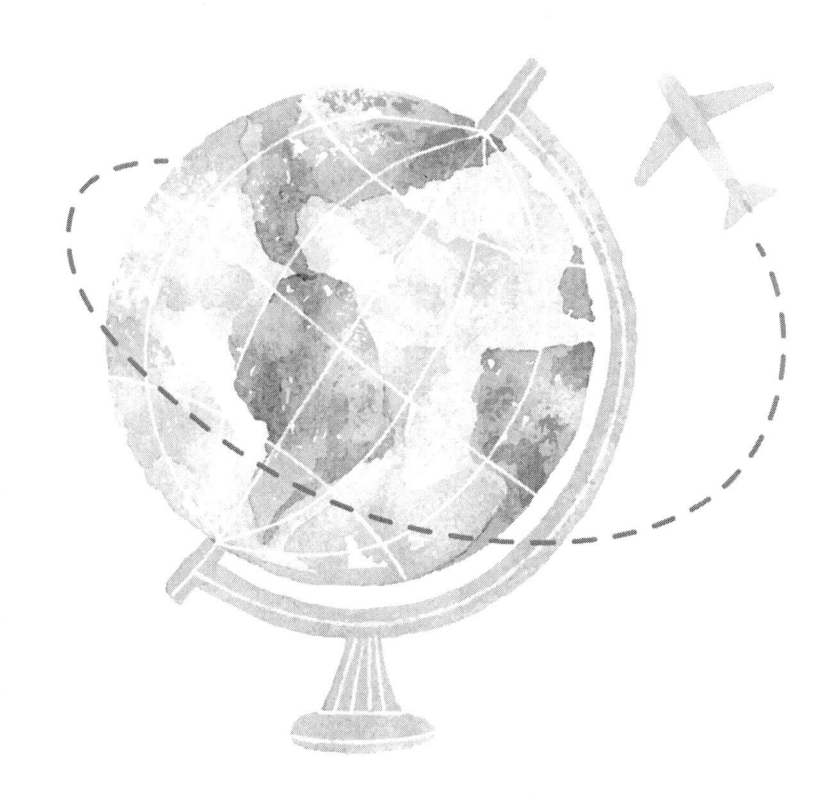

Table of Contents

Prologue	1
1. Welcome to New Orleans	7
2. Flight to Italy	13
3. Making Lemonade Out of Lemons	19
4. The Motor Coach Shuffle	25
5. We Will Always Have Nantucket	33
6. Fly, Fly Away	41
7. Oh Canada	53
8. Tour Guide Gone Bad	61
9. Surprise Visitors	67
10. New York, New York's a Wonderful Town	75
11. Christmas Dreams Come True	81
Epilogue	85

Prologue

How did a girl who hailed from the Bronx, New York become a world traveler? Growing up we never travelled much. Being a city girl, my parents sent me to summer camp to escape the summer heat. That was my vacation. Up until I married my husband Jim, I had only visited three surrounding states, so you could say that my worldview was limited to what was familiar.

Things changed rather quickly for me once Jim and I were married. When we met, he was a cadet at West Point. I knew he would enter the army and go wherever the powers that be sent him. That undoubtedly would be out of my comfort zone. But then again, almost any location would be just that. When word came that we would be moving to Germany, I knew for sure that moving halfway around the world would be overwhelming, and I began to panic. I was not ready to live in a new culture so far away from family.

One experience almost derailed any chance of moving very far from home. Soon after we were married, Jim had to report to

Confessions of a Crazed Tour Guide

Fort Benning, Georgia, for a special nine-week school. We had taken an extra-long honeymoon driving across the country, and the trip would end in Georgia. The plan was for me to fly home to New York for the duration of the training.

Sounds like a great plan. Except I had never flown before and I was very nervous. It took days to convince me that I could do this. On the day I was to fly home, we arrived at the small airport in Columbus, Georgia, where the plane would make a connection in Atlanta to complete my journey to New York. Now this is ancient history for most folks, but there were no jetways in those days. We just opened the airport door and walked out onto the tarmac to the waiting plane. Suddenly the two-engine prop looked huge, and my fears resurfaced. Jim calmed my nerves by walking me onto the plane—believe me, once upon a time you could actually do this. I was able to choose my seat. Jim pointed to a window seat right over the wing. "Most comfortable seat on the plane!" Jim exclaimed. With a big hug and kiss, he said goodbye and sadly walked off the plane. My heart began to beat rapidly, and my hands were sweaty. I felt so alone. Would I be able to navigate the Atlanta airport to reach my connecting flight? So hesitantly I took my seat, looked out the plane window, and tried to talk myself out of all those nervous butterflies I was feeling. Before long, a very nice woman sat next to me, and we got to talking. Soon the noisy engines seemed to rattle my seat as the plane took us down the runway. My sheer terror was subdued by the conversation with my seat mate.

Before I knew it, we were in the air, and I was well on my way to my destination. At this point, things were going smoothly, and I began to wonder, *what could possibly go wrong?* Just as these thoughts swirled through my head, I glanced out the window. I had to blink twice to realize the reality of what I was seeing. To my utter horror, the engine right outside my window was on fire! I mean, balls of fire emanating from the engine. Just as I was processing what I had seen, the pilot announced, "Ladies and gentlemen, our engine is on fire! I am going to land the plane right here." From this point on, my memory is pretty sketchy. "What did he say?" I mumbled. I do not remember anyone answering me. My mind was a tumble of emotions, most of them being panic.

I wish I could tell you what happened next. I am not certain how I got out of the burning plane. My only remembrance is of the other passengers and me walking away from the plane. I found myself in a field of corn ripe enough to pick. The plane sat amidst the corn, looking almost otherworldly and grotesquely out of place. How was it that I was walking through a corn field in the middle of rural Georgia? Today it seems like an episode of *The Walking Dead*. Did we all look like zombies? I have no idea, but as if a mirage appeared before me, I saw an old general store. I, along with many others, slowly walked towards it, and I managed to mumble out the words, "Is there a phone?"

Nervously I called Jim's commanding officer and relayed my tale of horror. Of course, Jim came to my rescue as fast as he could, and we drove back to his army post. Both of us were in a haze wondering what to do next. Do I curl up in a ball and relive the nightmare I had just experienced, or do I press forward and make my way back home to wait for Jim's schooling to be completed? I could not sleep at all that night. I vacillated between panic and abject fear. How would I ever overcome this overwhelming dread of ever flying again?

Well, as with most things in life, a new morning brought a determination to complete the journey and prove to myself that I could do it. Once again, we made our way to the airport, and I boarded the plane with the hope of arriving safely back home. Had I begun to conquer my fear, or was I just learning to live with it? Only time would tell.

We slowly traversed the tarmac at the Columbus, Georgia, airport. My hands were shaking and I could barely put one foot in front of the other. Jim's hand guided me onto the waiting plane, and he gently led me to my seat. Soon, the engines fired up, and the old prop plane lumbered down the bumpy tarmac. In my head, I was making bargains with God while secretly hoping I would never have to be called to account. This time, the journey was much less traumatic, and before long, I returned to New York with the joy of touching terra firma. That is a feeling I will never forget.

Needless to say, since that fateful day, I have logged thousands of air miles. No flight ever came close to the sheer terror of that day. My decision to overcome my fear of flying has given way to a most amazing love of travel and a career that surprised me daily.

How is it possible I chose a career that would take me to many places around the world? It certainly is a circuitous route. After my initial flight almost ended in tragedy, I was forced to confront my fear of flying. Jim was a career army officer and his assignments took us both overseas and around our country. Our initial assignment was Germany. Obviously, there is a big ocean separating the United States and Germany. Navigating that reality took an emotional toll. I had to make a conscious decision to trust the pilot's expertise and hope like crazy all would be well.

I certainly did not start out in the world of travel. For many years, I worked in the field of education. Much of that time was spent with kindergarteners. Even so, I felt a tug towards switching gears and pursuing my education, studying history with an emphasis on tourism. Upon graduation, I reinvented myself, so to speak. I sought work as a tour guide. A local company decided to take a chance and hire me to escort seniors on motor coach trips throughout the area. I soon came to love both the fellow travelers and historic sights we visited. After several years of working for the travel company, I realized I could be the master of my fate. I decided to branch out and form my own company. I had a wonderful partner, Margaret, and together we grew a great and loyal following. Just after Margaret retired, I was approached by a large organization to produce all the tours for their senior citizens. This opportunity led to hundreds of trips spanning over twenty years. My company became the largest tour company in our region of Virginia.

This book is replete with true accounts of my life as a world-traveling tour guide. There was no need to embellish any of these stories. Most are almost too crazy to believe, but I assure you each chapter is an accurate description of each trip. Only the names have been changed to protect the guilty.

1

Welcome to New Orleans

"June, come quickly! Violet has just fallen down the escalator!" Welcome to New Orleans and what proves to be a more insane trip than I ever could have imagined.

After all, we are about to board the *Mississippi Queen* for a lovely, restful river cruise.

And such is the life of a tour guide. Expect the unexpected, keep calm in the face of crisis, and never let them see you sweat. Now, I must tell you that this is my first experience taking a group out of our local area. I have never flown with a group before, let alone led them on a week-long adventure. I am assured it will be easy, a piece of cake, no problem. It should be an exciting trip. Having never been to New Orleans, I soon realize that life will get more complicated than I ever could have imagined. Since this is a group of aging seniors, each traveler is simply one misstep away from potential disaster. With that realization, I now know my travel life is never going to be easy or a piece of cake.

Soon after the plane lands, I sprint ahead to the baggage claim to help the cruise representative mark our luggage for our River Extravaganza. Each one of my thirty travelers is ready to board a Southern Paddlewheel boat and marvel at the many historic points along the Mighty Mississippi. "The cruise of a lifetime" is the familiar refrain. My merry band of silver-hair adventurers are anxious to set sail. Their eagerness is tempered by a bit of nervousness. For many, this flight and cruise is a first-time experience. I explain to each one that I must go ahead of them to meet the cruise envoy. "Please take the elevator down one level" is my plea. After all, no one in the group would take a chance on navigating a steep escalator in a strange airport.

I faintly hear my name being called, but this couldn't possibly be one of my octogenarian charges. I am surrounded by a sea of luggage as I receive instructions from the cruise representative. Coming to my senses and realizing that I was indeed being summoned, I jerk my head to the left and, sure enough, there is ninety-one-year old Violet sprawled out at the base of the moving stairs. "Violet, are you ok?" I inquire. *What a stupid question.* Undoubtedly, she is not ok. She is screaming in pain as the EMT's came scurrying out of the woodwork. I instantly know what was in my future: a little trip to New Orleans' finest general hospital.

Now there is the small matter of dealing with the thirty others travelers who have joined me on this voyage up the mighty

Mississippi. How am I going to get them to the ship and Violet to the hospital at the same time? As usual, it is just me shepherding another silver-hair bevy of seniors on another exciting adventure, and I am wishing I could be in two places at once (as most great guides can do).

Think, June, think. What now? Much to my relief, the river cruise envoy comes to my aid and says, "I'll take the rest of the group to the river boat while you go to the hospital with Violet."

"Oh joy, there is nothing I would rather do!" I declare as I curse this unfortunate event and what is about to happen.

Before you can say "Mardi Gras," an ambulance zips to the airport entrance. Now, Violet is on a gurney and being loaded into the waiting vehicle. I now have to bid farewell to the rest of the group and promise I will see them on board our floating vacation cruise in just a little while.

Ha! Don't be so sure. I am about to enter the alternate universe of an inner city hospital emergency room. Violet is in pain and *quickly* needs an X-ray to determine the extent of her injury. Did I say quickly? Well, that term is relative. What is fast for you and me could be slow as molasses in January for others. It seems this fine emergency room subscribes to the latter. Movements are so slow that slow motion looks speedy. Medical personnel seem to be non-existent, or perhaps they are off taking a little nap. What's the hurry? The clock is ticking in real time, and as minutes turn to hours I see no progress in X-raying Violet. I am now pacing the hall when I spy a doctor moving more slowly than Tim Conway's little old man. I seize the opportunity to grab onto his lapels and utter the words, "I have 1,500 passengers waiting for us at the *Mississippi Queen*! I need to know if her hip is broken and soon!" The guy has a glazed look in his eyes, but I may have gotten through to him. Perhaps he hears the urgency in my voice. Maybe he discerns my concern for Violet as well as my duties as guide-in-chief to thirty waiting travelers aboard our river boat. Did I make a breakthrough? Nothing to do now but wait.

As I sit not-so-patiently in the waiting area, I am seated next to a worried family and am treated to one of the oddest conversations I have ever had the privilege of overhearing. "Why, I swear I don't know how that knife got in his shoulder! It must have just come down from heaven and that's where it landed!" Now I know I have officially entered the "twilight zone." Not only am I in a freak show of a hospital, but my group waiting on the riverboat may well leave without me! How did I ever get in this mess? My first long trip as a tour guide could well be an utter failure. Will the riverboat sail without me? Will I leave the rest of my group in the lurch? I am a novice at this. I may just fail at my first real test of group travel.

At six o'clock in the evening, I make a bold move. I decide to bet on the fact that Violet's hip is not broken. I call a taxi. It is now one hour until the ship sails!

At 6:10, an unnamed doctor greets me with the words, "Her hip is not broken, only bruised." This is music to my ears. Now, faster than a speeding bullet, I literally start throwing Violet's clothing back on. Trust me there is no particular order. I don't care if her bra goes on last. When you have eight layers of undetermined undergarments, there is no way to figure out the order, but at this moment my only thought is to get the heck out of there. Violet seems a bit dazed and confused but is willing to go along with my plan. She is now seated in a wheel chair, and at breakneck speed, I wheel her to the exit. Like a miracle from Heaven, a taxi arrives at the door. I ask a stranger if this is my taxi. He replies, "Lady! I would take it, since cabs never come here." Ok! We are off! Violet has been loaded in the cab—complete with various garments that I knew not where they went.

"Hurry!" I yell to the driver as we speed through New Orleans. Faster than a running back heading for the goal line, we drive through parts unknown, and I am just praying this driver is not taking us on a wild goose chase. I am making bargains with God that could never be fulfilled, but hey, I am desperate.

Do I see the outline of a paddle wheel boat off in the distance? Have we defied the odds? As I am thinking these thoughts, we arrive at the cruise location. Prayers of thanks seem inadequate. We come to a screeching halt, and Violet and I pile out of the cab. I must have won the good luck lottery.

At 6:57 p.m., we pull up to our river boat. As we exit the taxi, we are greeted by 1,500 passengers all standing on the deck and cheering Violet and me on our arrival. Now that is how you make an entrance and gain attention!

Confessions of a Crazed Tour Guide

Violet is safely on board. I am as well. I head straight for the bar and order the biggest glass of wine they have. Somehow, when I agreed to be a tour guide, none of this was in the job description. Tomorrow is another day, and time to do it all again.

ROME

2

Flight to Italy

Arrivederci! Italy here we come. My husband Jim and I are bringing another stalwart group of intrepid travelers across the "pond," this time to sunny Italy. Now, I have to tell you that I love the folks who trust me and will go anywhere just on my say so. What faith. All I have to do is to live up to their expectations, and that is where the rubber meets the road. When taking large groups to Europe, I partner with a larger tour company. We can join one of their prearranged tours. It usually works out quite well, and I can count on them to handle most of the arrangements. Once in Italy, their guide greets our group and takes over the organization and tour guiding. It is a win-win for all.

Did I happen to mention that some of these travelers require more hand holding and patience than others? Well, this would be a good time to get you acquainted with Kelly. We go way back! One of my more faithful Trekkies, Kelly is an adventurous traveler, and she has specifically requested this trip. Even so, she can be a bit quirky and unpredictable. There are times when I do a lot of reassuring. I wonder if this would be the case on this multi-day tour. That should contextualize the events surrounding this foray into European travel.

Jim and I always get to the airport bright and early so that we can help folks check in at the agent counter. For this particular trip, we are positioned at the airline desk ready to greet our many travelers. One by one, everyone begins to arrive, and we are feeling good. But Kelly and her partner have not been seen, and now I am getting worried. Where could she be? After a little arm-twisting from the agent, we find out they have already checked in and have gone through security. Wow! Guess we were not early enough. If there is one thing I have learned from traveling with seniors, it is that, however early you are, someone has beaten you to the punch.

Well then, nothing to do but "sally forth," as they say, and proceed to the gate. Like the Pied Piper, I encourage our group of thirty to follow us up the escalator and through security. Of course, this involves various stages of undress and security wands in strange and unusual places. We endure this because the end result is going to be great. This will be a delightful trip to a beautiful country. What could go wrong?

As we walk up to our departure gate, I am greeted by Kelly's ever vigilant partner, Meg. Meg is salt of the earth and not prone to becoming worried or overwrought. We usually leave that all up to Kelly. Meg greets us with a grim look of concern and ushers us over to Kelly. I'm not prepared for what I see. Her face is puffy, swollen, and drooping on one side. This looks very serious to me, and she is definitely not in a condition fit for flying overseas.

"Kelly, what has happened to you?" I inquire. As I ask the question, I am already thinking about the many ways I can get Kelly to sack the itinerary and go home.

"I have Bell's palsy. The doctor has given me the green light to go, and I have all my medications," says Kelly. She tells me all this as if it is reasonable and what everyone else would do.

Are you kidding me? She now looks like a prize fighter on steroids. I have thirty other travelers needing my attention, but now I am focused in on just one. If you think this is the first time this has happened, you would be mistaken.

"Kelly, please call your husband. He can come back to the airport and take you home. This trip is too risky and long to leave in your condition." This is not an unreasonable request. Most people would have hightailed it for home, but Kelly is agitated and not thinking clearly. "I can't have Dave come back." She says. "He would kill me! I have to go, and you know I feel fine."

Right! Kelly now looks like a blowfish, and I can tell she is sick. What's a tour guide to do? As I am contemplating my dwindling options, I hear the attendant start announcing the boarding process. My sick traveler stands up to board, and I already know this is going to be a very long flight and trip. Man, I do not get paid enough! Kelly is determined to take this trip, and she is now boarding the plane. I am left feeling helpless. No amount of dissuasion is making a dent, including the promise of a refund if she does not board the plane. All logic is to no avail. Kelly is determined to see the statue of David, the Colosseum, and all the historic sites that Italy has to offer. What I had originally thought was going to be a fun adventure to the land of DaVinci, Michelangelo, and gorgeous architecture has now taken on a feeling of dread, making me wish I was anywhere else but on a plane to Italy.

Long flights only seem longer when met with the feeling of impending doom! *Lord, just get us to Rome* is my only prayer. I work off my anxiousness by stalking Kelly as I pace up and down the narrow aisle of the plane; I'm getting my exercise, I tell her. In reality, I am trying to figure out if her blowfish-like facial qualities are getting better or worse. The hours drone on, and the plane can't land soon enough! My faithful traveler now looks pale, and I know what is coming. Then, I am ushered to my seat as I hear the captain telling everyone to remain in their seats. Oh joy, the waiting game is on. Only one hour until we land in Rome, where I can get Kelly safely to our hotel and into the waiting arms of another guide who will be with us for the remainder of the trip. Then, I am off the hook, and let the chips fall where they may.

Just as I am reassuring myself, I hear an announcement over the loudspeaker. "Is there a doctor on board?" Oh no, that call couldn't possibly be for Kelly, could it? No, couldn't be. Like a jack rabbit on the hunt, the person next to me jumps up! "I am a doctor," he declares. As I watch him go up the aisle, I see him stop at a familiar row. Yep. You guessed it. Kelly is sick as a dog, and something tells me that this is going to be a very long day. We can't land soon enough. Kelly is vomiting violently and having trouble breathing. Did I mention that she has a heart condition that presents its own problems? Things are going from bad to worse when we begin our descent. As soon as we land, EMTs come on board. Kelly is placed on a stretcher, and her partner and I go along with her to the clinic at the airport. The rest of the travelers meet our Italy guide and head to the hotel. I see a pattern here. Once again, my group has gone without me, and I am left to deal with a sick passenger.

Anyone know Italian? Not me. I can't communicate with the clinic staff, but they have given Kelly an IV of something or other, and Meg and I just sit and wait. We are both exhausted, having been up all night, and the thought of a warm, comfy bed sounds very appealing. As I daydream about my cozy bed, the clinic staff reports that they have done all they can do. We can take her to the hotel and wait it out.

Now, we are in a strange city, and I have no clue how to get to our hotel. The only answer is a taxi cab that will cost seventy-five U.S. dollars and eat up whatever euros I have. Meg and I pile Kelly in the cab (once again, do you see a pattern developing?). We fly through the streets of Rome and play chicken with one scooter after another. If I wasn't so worried about Kelly's deteriorating condition, I may well have had a heart attack maneuvering the crazy streets of Rome. Eventually, we arrive at the hotel, and Meg and I take Kelly to her room and place her in her bed.

The good news is that the guide who works for the tour company I have partnered with will be with us throughout Italy and will take over Kelly duties from here. Kelly is in bed and not getting any better. I continue to check on her while we are in Rome. Poor girl is feeling worse. The only solution is to send her back to the United States just twenty-four hours after arriving in Italy.

We make a call to her husband to alert him of Kelly's early return. We all arrange a flight back to the States for her, and I pray the agents will let her on the plane and not think she has a communicable disease ready to spread to other travelers. Meg and I bid Kelly a sad farewell and reassure her that all will be well. Now the guide from the tour company takes her to the Rome airport and convinces one and all that Kelly is right as rain and fit to fly.

If there is one thing that tour guides know how to do, it is how to throw the bull around so that it sounds perfectly logical and reasonable. Once in New York, her husband meets Kelly, and once home, she is able to get the treatment that puts her on the road to recovery. Unbelievable. Once again, the unthinkable becomes a reality.

3
Making Lemonade Out of Lemons

Through the years, I have had the pleasure of visiting many beautiful cities in the U.S. None are lovelier than Charleston, South Carolina. It is a vision of antebellum mansions and welcoming porches which both cool the houses and add charm. The rows of sherbet-colored homes delight the eyes. One can easily envision fine Southern ladies walking along the historic Battery with splendid water views of the Ashley and Cooper Rivers. The city just oozes charm. I never get tired of visiting Charleston.

This is a good thing since I often bring groups to Charleston. During my early years of travel, I was asked by my employer to bring a group here. So much to see. It is a history buff's mecca. I am awed by the many historic structures that stand tall amidst the church steeples on almost every corner. Many times, I have strolled the quaint, brick-lined streets soaking in the sights and sounds of the Battery, the open-air market, and the majestic homes that seem to beckon me to come in and stay a while. This is Southern elegance at its finest. Everyone's favorite locale.

Whenever I am asked to accompany a group to Charleston, I almost have to pinch myself. Could there be a better occupation? Before each trip, I immerse myself in learning as much as possible about each location, and Charleston is no exception. This is my equivalent to cramming for a final.

As the time draws near for us to depart, I am filled with nervous anticipation. Since this is before the start of my own company, I did not make any of the arrangements for our multi-day tour of the "holy city," as Charleston is sometimes called. I am given reams of notes, hotel and restaurant contracts, and every other item I need to make this a terrific getaway. My supervisor has filled me in on all the pertinent materials, and I am armed with a head full of knowledge and a feeling of anticipation.

All I have to do is carry out the perfect plan. But that is usually easier said than done. Before cell phones and instant communication, I was usually on my own with paper maps—this is prior to the days of GPS—as my only guiding lights. The morning of the tour begins very early. I must prepare the coach with all the "valuables": snacks, supplies, and of course, the mountains of paperwork necessary to ensure a successful journey. Before long, my eager group of travelers begin boarding our rolling "fun zone."

How does one keep about forty passengers happy and engaged for a long journey? You have lots of food and beverages along with a healthy dose of bus games. Making the time go quickly is one of my specialties. It is about seven hours from southern Virginia to Charleston. I have to keep my merry band of travelers busy during our ride. We play games, give out prizes, and eat a myriad of snacks. So, by the time we get to our destination, the natives are getting restless, so to speak. They are more than eager to get to our historic Charleston hotel.

My directions say that we are staying at a Holiday Inn close to the Charleston airport. Directions in hand, our driver makes his way to the designated hotel. It is always quite a relief to arrive at our destination. The hotel looks nice enough, so I disembark the coach first and announce our arrival to the waiting hotel staff. Once in the lobby, I introduce myself to the desk clerk and tell him the bus group has arrived. He looks at me with a curious gaze and a quizzical look. He replies, "What tour group?" Now, I am really confused. Nowhere in his books is there a reservation for a tour group, and the hotel is all but sold out for the night. There definitely are not twenty extra rooms available. What's an ace tour guide to do?

"There must be some mistake!" I say. "I have forty tired and hungry travelers on the coach, and we must have a resolution to this dilemma."

The hotel clerk is just as confused as I am. Since my motto is "Never let them see you sweat," I am not about to let on to the group that there is a potential disaster unfolding. *Think, June, think.* I must come up with a plan, and the clock is ticking. First things first: my group is hungry, and they need to eat. There is a restaurant attached to the hotel. This is akin to finding a mirage in the middle of the desert. Emergency plan one: food usually can mollify the most disgruntled traveler.

I decide to board the coach and announce that we will have dinner at this fine dining establishment. Surprisingly, no one questions this choice, and emergency plan one is off to a good start. All folks exit the coach and are soon chowing down on their impromptu meal. Meanwhile, I am trying to sort out the current mess. Let's review: I am in Charleston with forty travelers who are expecting to stay at this hotel, and there is literally "no room at the inn!" What to do?

Now, the hotel clerk has an idea. He tells me that all reservations go through a central office for all Holiday Inns in the area. Could it be that the person who put this trip together made the reservation at a different Holiday Inn and sent me to the wrong hotel? A couple of phone calls later and the mystery has been solved. Yes, indeed, a Holiday Inn closer to downtown Charleston is awaiting our arrival. What a relief! Now all I have to do is figure out a way to save face. Time to implement emergency plan two.

Do I dare tell them that we stopped at the wrong hotel? Am I pushing my luck? As folks are finishing up their dinner, I saunter into the restaurant and announce, "How would you like to stay at a hotel closer to Charleston?" As I wait for their response, my knees begin to buckle, and my heart rate quickens.

Soon, I hear a rumble forming. It is soft at first but rising quickly. Cheers go up from the crowd. This is music to their ears. It seems I have caught a break. I begin to unclench my teeth and relax my shoulders. Things seem to be looking up. Could this crazy dilemma be coming to an end?

"I have awesome news for you! All you have to do is get back on the coach, and away we will go!" I exclaim. "I have secured you space at one of the nicest hotels in the heart of Charleston."

As my newly happy band of very tired travelers board the coach, there are no complaints from the group, only praise that I made the impossible happen. As we get closer to Charleston, I can hear an excited hum emanating from the group. With each passing historic building, cheers sound even louder. Before long, our lovely downtown hotel comes into view. The hotel is infinitely better. Its historic charm matches our surroundings. Each traveler thanks me for pulling off this feat. Now, I am a hero! The whole trip is saved, and a sack of lemons has just been sweetened to make lemonade. Just another day on the job for Super Guide.

4

The Motor Coach Shuffle

Every trip is a new adventure, and the viability of the motor coach is always number one on my list of priorities for a successful trip. A motor coach is akin to a science experiment. It is part strategic planning, part road-worthiness, and part sheer good luck. You need all these components to make the dream trip a reality. I must admit that, most of the time, the buses I charter run just fine. Usually, there are no problems, and that part of the planning is one less thing to worry about. But then there are those times, always at the most inconvenient time and place, when the unthinkable happens. On one particular day, our group is heading towards the western part of Virginia to taste the wines of our region. Such fun. No stress, just visions of clinking glasses and sampling the best chardonnay the vineyard has to offer.

Nothing like getting underway with my group of hopeful travelers riding down the interstate at a cool sixty-five miles per hour, not a care in the world, when, all of a sudden, the engine of the coach begins to sputter, and our speed becomes a slow crawl down to first gear. Next thing you know, we are pulling to the side of the road, and we come to a screeching halt. Great! We are dead in the water, at a full stop with no hope of being at our destination on time. How does a tour guide manage this situation when the perfect plan turns into a mini nightmare? Keep cool, calm, and collected. Never panic; think fast, and spring into action. At this moment, I have one thought. My cell phone is my best friend, and an emergency call to the coach owner is first on my list. My pleading voice is begging for a magic bus to appear and jettison us out of this mess and put us back on track. We are not too far from home, and my sincerest hope is that the bus angels have miraculously done the impossible.

    The real trick is keeping the folks reassured while I am in panic mode the whole time. Now, that is a trick I have perfected. Waiting patiently is not my greatest virtue, but my performance is worthy of an Oscar. Murmurings begin at the rear of the coach and filter forward. "What is happening?" "How much longer?" "We want some answers." As if I had the perfect answer to these questions. I decide to quickly redial the bus company for an update. My hands are sweating, and my heart is racing. Have my travelers seen the beads of sweat forming on my brow? It is at times like these that I tend to reassess my life choices. Ok! One more phone call to the stalwart company owner, and as I dial, I pray earnestly that we have a resolution to this dilemma.

I can see the worried expressions on the faces of my fun bunch. Furrowed brows and anxious voices say it all. I need help now. My hands are shaking as I hear the coach owner's voice saying he has good news. *Did I hear correctly? Could it be true?* Could my mini nightmare be coming to an end? I hear the words "Another coach is on its way." I can honestly say the forty pound weight that I had on my shoulders seems to melt away like ice on a hot summer day. Prayers of thanks seem inadequate. I then make a quick call to the winery to assure them that we will be there as soon as possible.

Next, I turn my attention to my jittery travelers. "Get ready to clink glasses in celebration. A rescue bus is coming our way, and the winery is ready and waiting," I say. Cheers swell up from the group. Thank goodness they are flexible and accommodating. Just one more prayer answered.

* * *

You would think this would be a one-time occurrence, but sadly it is not. No perfect plan ever comes off without a hitch.

It is the day of a big holiday party, and I am coordinating buses that are taking over 250 seniors to this event. I secure the right number of coaches and make sure that each pickup location has enough coordinators to help each traveler get safely onto the bus. Since each coach has to make multi stops, timing is key.

Confessions of a Crazed Tour Guide

One fly in the ointment can upend everything. Plans have been in place for a while, and at first, all is going well. One coach is coming from the furthest point and then picking up more travelers at another stop before coming to the big holiday luncheon. Sounds like a great plan; works for me. That is, until I get a call from coach owner Dan. Hum! He tells me that as the bus was coming to the second stop, it developed engine trouble and is currently sitting on the side of the road. There are many folks already on board, and they are cold and getting hungrier by the minute. Unfortunately, this coach is supposed to be on the way to the second pick up, and it cannot get there. Uh oh! Those would-be merry makers are waiting in the cold at stop number two, and the coach is nowhere in sight. Yes, that's right; it is on the side of the road sitting motionless. Now, I have to figure out just how I can rescue the stranded partygoers and pick up those still waiting. This is like a bad dream that keeps repeating itself. Once again, my pulse quickens, and my throat is dry. Another familiar feeling of dread overtakes me. What is a stalwart tour operator supposed to do when the present situation seems out of my control? Panic? Scream, "why me?" Not if I can help it.

The time seems to be slipping away. I decide to make one more frantic call to the coach owner. Help. "What are we going to do? How can this problem be solved?" I implore. I am picturing shivering seniors waiting outside and helpless party goers worried as they sit by the side of the road. Thoughts of the Grinch stealing Christmas whirl through my head. I am almost at my wits end and panic is evident in my voice. My stalwart owner reassures me that he has a plan. Faster than you can say Merry Christmas, another bus is being dispatched, not only to rescue the folks on the side of the road but also to pick up the last stragglers at the second pick up location. At this moment, my nerves calm down. *Why was I so worried?* I remind myself that being in charge is not all it is cracked up to be. Pacing nervously is what I do best. The doors to the holiday luncheon are opening to the awaiting guests. I just hope the stragglers are not too late to enjoy the festivities. I nervously walk up and down the sidewalk and look for any hopeful sign. Out of the corner of my eye, I spy a beautiful white coach coming into view. Yes, it has all the stranded riders more than ready for a celebration. This tale may have a happy and merry ending, but I now know that each of these "little" episodes are taking years off my already dwindling life. Today was one of those days when no truer words have been spoken.

* * *

Well, you would think that would be the end of it. What more could happen? At this point I would swear that I had seen it all.

If you, too, are thinking that same thing, then you have another thing coming. It is that time of year again. Fall is in the air, and a trip north to New England is just what the doctor ordered. Nothing like brisk, cool air to liven the spirits and tickle the senses. I am most fortunate to have eager travelers that flock to our annual autumn get away. My spirit is always renewed by the prospect of spying majestic leaves turning deep gold, bright yellow, and vibrant red. I can almost taste the sweet, delicious apples and crisp cider. Ah, the wonder of it all. To think, I am able to accompany a group on such a journey—what a special privilege.

On one such trip, we begin day one in a fine mood. The coach is full, and excitement is evident as each traveler boards the New England express. Everyone on board shares my delight and sense of adventure. We are off to a great start. There is little traffic as we head north, and I am counting my lucky stars that all is well. Since we are making good time, I decide to stop for an early lunch. We just happen to find a great location. We are at a restaurant adjacent to a shopping mall. You know what that means. When travelers spy shopping, they are eager to dive right in. "Can we have extra time?" come the pleas from the ladies in the group. "Sure. Why not," I say. "Take a little longer. No worries."

My eager group scurries off the coach to grab lunch and a bargain or two at one of the many stores while I take a few minutes to eat and hurry back to the bus. Once on board, I see my driver with a worried expression on his face. Did I hear correctly? "Did I just hear you say that you can't restart the bus? That can't be!" I exclaim. We have just begun a week-long adventure, and we have miles to go before we sleep. The tell-tale signs of stress reappear. I am sweating now, and my heart is pounding. My bad dream seems to play out over and over again. This can't be happening. What to do? Once again, I am making frantic phone calls. Soon, over forty travelers will reappear. What will I say? What can I do?

The bus company is under the gun again. They have to produce a coach for the remainder of the day. We are due at our dinner and hotel within a few hours, and time is of the essence. My nerves are on edge as my group wanders back to the waiting coach.

I have to be the bearer of bad news. I tentatively relay the upsetting information that we are literally at a standstill. Nervous chatter reverberates throughout the grounded bus. What can I say to alleviate concerns? As my mind scrambles for just the right thing to say, my driver calls me aside. As if witnessing a miracle, the driver tells me that we have secured a new coach. It will be arriving in about an hour. The bad news is that the driver and I must transfer all the contents of our coach onto the new one. Never did I think I would be saved by a shopping mall. I send my leaf peepers back to the mall while we wait for the bus to appear. Yea. Before too long, the gleaming new ride comes into view. My driver and I express our thanks for the new driver's swift appearance, and we all begin tossing luggage under the new coach and loading supplies on the bus.

Well, better late than never. Eventually, we are once again off, heading to our waiting restaurant and hotel. I must say, that evening food never tasted so good, and the bed seems to beckon. Oh, the highs and lows of just one day in the life of a tour guide.

5

We Will Always Have Nantucket

There is no better tradition in the hallowed halls of travel than the fabled annual trek to New England in the fall. Beautiful and majestic scenery, the thrill of vibrant colored leaves, and the chill that warms your heart as the air feels crisp and the blue skies seem even more azure than usual. It is here that I take my eager group each October.

It all sounds so idyllic, doesn't it? A coachload of eager travelers heading north to take in the full effect of nature at its finest.

Well, if it all sounds too good to be true, that is because it is. As I may have mentioned before, I am blessed to have many faithful friends who trust me to guide them expertly from one point of interest to the next. It is on just one such trip that my story takes a most unbelievable turn.

Where do I begin? Kate has traveled with me for many years. To say that she is somewhat persnickety is a complete understatement. Time after time, she has been a thorn in my side, a force to be reckoned with. Crossing Kate has its consequences. She could stop you dead in your tracks with an icy stare or cut you down with one caustic remark. Yet she constantly professes her undying devotion to me. Lately, Kate's behavior has become more erratic. Out of the blue, she would become highly agitated, making sure others around her feel uncomfortable and downright resentful that she is part of the trip.

Before our New England trip begins, I decide to contact Kate and ascertain just how mentally alert she is. If I think she is mentally unable to travel, I am going to lower the proverbial boom. "No trip for you" will be my swift reply. I am going to be firm. But the more we talk, I wonder if her erratic behavior is a figment of my imagination. She seems fine. Fit as a fiddle. Darn! Now, I have to accept the inevitable. I decide to call my helper and dear friend Pat. "I am so happy you are coming with me because I sure do need your help with a thorny problem. How would you like to babysit Kate so her behavior does not get out of hand?" I ask. Pat's response is a hearty chuckle and a quick yes, knowing the restraint and patience it will take to keep Kate happy.

The day soon arrives for our big trip. I meet the coachload of happy and excited travelers. Everyone is looking forward to seeing scenic Cape Cod and Nantucket Island, such iconic parts of New England. This is a place where the fall air feels especially refreshing. Seafood is abundant, and the scenery is unmatched. Travelers are busy buzzing with one another in fervent anticipation, and I am thinking to myself that we are off to a great start.

Pat is diligent in her duties, and Kate has been subdued. The only indication that all may not be entirely well is hearing her bicker with her long-suffering husband and companion, Ben. Like the buzzing of a mosquito close to your ear, Kate's shrill voice gives rise to an uneasy sense that we may be in for a bumpy ride.

After two days of traveling, we arrive in Hyannis, Massachusetts. This was the home of President Kennedy. How lucky are we to visit his library and catch a glimpse of the family compound! Life is good as my trusty travelers board the ferry that will transport us to historic Nantucket Island. An expert local guide accompanies us for the day. She shares with us the rich history of one of the first island settlements in America. What a perfect day. The sun is bright, and the fall air makes me feel energized. The boat ride over is a bit bumpy, but my intrepid travelers are not deterred. In a corner of the ferry, I spy Kate and her husband, Ben. As usual, she is grousing about something, but I ignore her buzzing and take a seat.

Land ho! Before long we arrive on the island. Our guide gives us time to eat lunch at one of the local restaurants. Of course, lobster rolls are the island specialty. We are advised to go to different establishments so one is not overloaded. After lunch, we will all meet back up for an eagerly anticipated tour.

With the taste of lobster rolls on the mind, Pat and I make a beeline for one of the more popular eateries. Yum! This will taste so good and it will help make our trip complete. We are just about ready to order when one of my travelers comes running into the restaurant. "Come quickly; Ben has been arrested!" she exclaims. *What?* I think to myself, *this can't be.* Ben is a gentleman in his eighties and seems so gentle. I collect my jacket and purse, and now, I am running at warp speed to the scene of the crime, so to speak. When I arrive, I meet Officer Matt, who is in the process of handcuffing Ben and putting him in the back of a police car. It seems as though Ben and Kate were arguing outside a restaurant, and in his desire to push her away, he raised his hand and hit her in the eye. Oh my, battery charges are in his future, and a terrible day is in mine!

This must be a bad dream, I think to myself. This could not be happening. After all, I am on a small island with over fifty travelers who entrust me with a once-in-a-lifetime experience. I am determined not to let my fellow tourists see the ensuing spectacle. Fortunately, as I look around, I do not find my crew anywhere. Pat springs into action and makes a beeline for Kate. Of course, Kate is hysterical, agitated, and beyond reason. Pat is able to get her to an inside location while I have a little conversation with Officer Matt. Question number one: "How long will Ben be in your county jail?" Now, I am expecting to hear a week or longer, but no—it seems he will be arraigned in ninety minutes and bail will be set.

In all my years of leading groups, I have never encountered this scenario. The solution to this dilemma is not in any of my textbooks. My head is spinning with thoughts of impending tour chaos. What is the next logical step? I contemplate my very few options and snap back to reality. Fortunately, Pat has calmed Kate down enough to get her to drink something while we plot our next move! Our strategy is to keep Kate out of sight as much as possible. I learn that Ben is going to be transferred to the court house for arraignment, so we decide to escort a shaky Kate there. We each take one of her arms and swiftly whisk her down the street to the Nantucket Courthouse. As we are traversing the street, I look side to side to make sure none of my other travelers are within sight. Fortunately for us, the coast is clear, and before long, we arrive and seat Kate on a bench. She begins to weep once again, and Pat quiets her while I go looking for the bailiff. By the way, how did my idyllic day devolve into this scenario? Oh well, no time to reflect on what a mess this day has become; I have a job to do. Before long, I find the bailiff sitting at his desk. He explains to me that Ben will be brought over to the court house in about an hour. At that time, he can post bail of forty dollars and be on his merry way. *Oh joy!* I think to myself. *Now what?*

    I have to come up with a plan to rid myself and our fellow travelers of Kate and Ben. This will not be easy, but I often do my best thinking in times of extreme stress. My alter ego, "Super Guide," springs into action. Quickly, I call my husband, Jim. "When is the next ferry off this island?" I ask. Jim is aware of my predicament and is already on the case. Fortunately for me, the next ferry is going to work. I am going to make certain that the "dynamic duo" is on that ferry. Then, I ask Jim to call a car rental agency to have a car waiting at the ferry landing for Ben and Kate. The master plan is to have them collect their belongings and drive off before the rest of the group returns to Hyannis. All that is left to do is tell the happy couple that they have been voted off the island!

Well, time is speeding along, and Kate seems less anxious. She is sitting quietly awaiting Ben's newfound freedom. Fearing that Kate's emotional state cannot quite handle the eventual termination from the trip, I have not yet spoken with her. Instead, Pat keeps her preoccupied. We are plotting our next move as I spot a handcuffed Ben accompanied by two police officers coming right toward us. Uh oh! I was hoping to avoid this sight. I do not want to upset Kate more. But Kate sees them coming our way and shrieks in horror. Great! Just what we need, unglued Kate and handcuffed Ben. This scenario is not in the plan. In fact, I could never imagine that such a thing could happen. Pat is once again charged with calming down our shaky client. I, on the other hand, am off to check on how bail is progressing.

Ah, life on a small island. What am I to do when my traveler has been arrested and is posting the "enormous sum" of forty dollars for bail? I have entered an altered state at this moment. A million thoughts are swirling in my head all at once. *How do I keep this incident from infecting our trip like a rare virus? Can I actually make them leave on the next ferry? Is there any way to walk them through the town of Nantucket without my group realizing Kate and Ben are "walking the plank?"*

A voice from one of the police officers brings me back to reality. He informs me the judge only comes once a week. He will not return for another ten days, so we are informed that Ben can leave as long as he returns to appear before the judge at his appointed date. Interesting! As the police share this with Ben and remove his handcuffs, I can see his mental wheels turning. Now is the moment for me to drop the hammer. I say, "Ben, you and Kate cannot continue on this trip with us." Then, I hear a very loud shriek coming from behind me. Why, of course it is Kate, thunderstruck at this news. But I am strong and will not be swayed. Nothing they can say will dissuade me from walking them swiftly to the boat dock.

Ben is unusually quiet as we walk out of sight of fellow travelers. Along the way, I share with Ben that, once back in Hyannis, a car will be waiting for them both. They are to quickly remove their things from the hotel and be on their merry way, never to be seen again. Ben nods and seems to agree with this decision.

I stand at the dock for quite a while and wait until they are on board the ferry. Good riddance! These two almost ruined a perfectly great New England Fall Foliage Tour, but thankfully, none of my dear charges are any the wiser. The next day, we are off to our next stop, free from drama and intrigue. The life of a guide is rarely easy, nor is it without struggles along the way. This day is proof of that.

6
Fly, Fly Away

Now, I am a seasoned traveler. I have accompanied many groups to a great many parts of the United States and Europe. With all that experience, another overseas adventure seems like a fine idea. One of the itineraries I have been dreaming about was a Baltic cruise. Since I am of Norwegian ancestry, I am anxious to once again explore my family's homeland. Jim busily researches various itineraries and comes up with the perfect plan. We are going to offer back-to-back, week-long cruises that depart from Copenhagen. Excitement is building as we explore the ports of call. What could be better than seeing cultural gems like Tallinn, Estonia, St. Petersburg, Russia, and other historic sites that border the majestic Baltic Sea? Sailing along the coast of Norway will be an exciting adventure for our second week long cruise. We will see beautiful fjords and visit several unique Norwegian villages. Homeland here I come.

Spread the word! Ads go out, and articles are written to encourage travelers to join us on this momentous voyage. Reservations come pouring in, and before we know it, over thirty travelers are ready to join us. What could be better? Sharing the joy of traveling to beautiful locations in Europe is what I live for. I can't imagine anything that can stop us from experiencing this part of the world.

Jim very carefully coordinates all the flight arrangements. At least ten folks are flying from around the country, but the bulk of the voyagers are departing from Southern Virginia. As you can imagine, all the travelers are arriving in Copenhagen at various times on day one. We have arranged for a local guide to meet our travelers, whisk them around Copenhagen, and drop them off safely at our hotel. We have planned to arrive a day before our cruise departure. This allows time to enjoy Copenhagen and recover from jet lag.

What, me? Worry? No way; we have anticipated just about everything. The only thing left to do is meet our travelers at the airport and board our plane for the trip of a lifetime.

An ominous call on the way to the airport is my first clue all would not go smoothly. A fellow traveler reports that our flight to JFK Airport has just been canceled and we are being rerouted to another airport. This proves to be the preamble to the dominoes falling one by one.

With the speed of light, we all but take flight for the remainder of the drive. Once at the airport, Jim and I work with the ticket agent to get us all on a new flight. As we work to find a good solution, our travelers begin to arrive. One by one, they gather. Now, it is up to me to share the concerning news. What is the best way to let our fellow travelers know that our flight has been cancelled? In addition, we say we must now fly to a different New York airport and, after arriving, make our way to JFK airport forty minutes away. It is difficult to put a positive spin on this development. Looks of worry and disbelief come over everyone's face. *Uh oh, could this possibly be happening now?* Why, we haven't even taken off yet. Mind you, we now are booked to arrive at La Guardia Airport in New York City. Our overseas connection is still taking off from JFK, so an added wrinkle greets us. The airlines promise us that transportation from one airport to the other will ensure that we make our flight. Promises, promises. Twenty-two of our travelers are with us while the remainder are blissfully unaware of our predicament.

    I am known for usually looking at the bright side of any situation. This, however, puts me to the ultimate test. In addition to moving with great haste to get us all through security in time to board the plane, ten of us do not make it on the plane. I see the large metal door close tightly. I feel defeated. Now, I am vacillating between despair and panic. How will our travelers already on the plane navigate all of this without us?

    We sit anxiously at the gate plotting our next move, and we notice that the plane to La Guardia with half my group does not move. Is this divine intervention? We have not had any communication with the airport staff at all. Ten of us feel alone and abandoned. Rarely have I felt so helpless. I am out of options, and right now, I envision our Baltic cruise will have to sail without us. Suddenly, the jet way door magically reopens. The flight attendant emerges to welcome us on board. Miracle number one!

It seems the plane has been delayed due to bad weather in New York. One of my fellow tourists has alerted the flight staff that the remainder of our group is stranded at the gate. Can this be true? I am astonished and grateful. The ten of us thankfully join the others on the plane.

The clock is ticking as we land at La Guardia. "Move as quickly as you can to retrieve your luggage," I say. We all look like a senior track team as we "beat feet" to baggage claim to meet our waiting transportation. It is a quarter past four, and our overseas flight is scheduled to leave at six o'clock. We quickly grab our luggage and head outside to our waiting van transportation. Surprise, there is no such van. No time to waste. Jim commandeers taxis for the group. We speed wildly through rush hour traffic. My heart is racing, and my teeth are clenched as I look at my watch for the twentieth time. Will we make it in time to board our overseas flight? As I am beginning to panic, we screech to a stop just outside of the arrivals section at the JFK airport. Have we made it on time? Will all be well?

We all rush to the check-in desk. We have forty-five minutes before departure. Phew. We made it! Finally, a stroke of good luck. Well, hang on to that thought. We have not counted on

"Frick and Frack" checking us in. Their counsel is that there is not enough time to make the flight. Are you kidding me? If we do not board the plane there will be twenty-two empty seats on that overseas flight. "Of course, you have to take care of my group," I say.

But no, they insist we cannot board. They offer no solutions to the problem of rerouting all of us. Panic and exhaustion are now evident on our travelers' faces, and the only hope of making this trip a reality is disappearing. How can we ever calm the storm of emotions and nerves under the circumstances?

One more time we attempt to talk with Frick and Frack to see if they can pull the proverbial rabbit out of the airline hat. We can see the agent frantically typing while attempting to correct our situation. After what seems like an eternity, they announce that they have space for five on a flight to Copenhagen through Amsterdam. Hurry, hurry, the plane is leaving in less than an hour. Some of my lucky travelers won the "golden ticket." I wish my friends well and say a silent prayer they make it safely to our destination. Off they go. Now, we are left with seventeen unlucky and unhappy souls. Any more miracles left for today? Believe me, we are praying for one, but so far, we are coming up short.

The rest of us stand at the counter in a stupor. Exhaustion overcomes us all. I am fresh out of ideas and any hopeful words. Then comes an announcement. Our agents have found seats on a morning Iceland Air flight. Too good to be true, but at least it is something. Jim and I have pulled many a rabbit out of a hat, so why would this situation be any different? Quickly, we secure hotel rooms for the group and bid them farewell. I personally accompany them to the hotel van. They seem relieved that another flight awaits them the next day. They are also aware that Jim and I will be departing on an Air France flight at midnight and that we will meet up again in Copenhagen. They are understanding of our predicament.

The same airport geniuses who booked Iceland Air also booked us on an Air France midnight flight through Paris. I am very skeptical. How can we leave the remainder of our travelers to an uncertain flight itinerary? They depend on us to be by their side. I am filled with worry and guilt. Leaving that evening seems unwise, to say the least. How will we all make it to Copenhagen in time for the cruise?

With much trepidation, we make our way to the Air France ticket agents. "Ready to board the flight to Paris!" we exclaim. Uh oh, a look of bewilderment on the faces of the agents makes me question whether we have a ticket at all. Soon, the word comes back to us. Ours is a standby ticket, and the flight is sold out. Lots of not-so-nice words come out of our mouths. We are assured we have seats on a flight the next afternoon. What is to become of us and our stranded travelers? A combination of disbelief and exhaustion engulfed us. By now, it is nearly midnight, and we must get some rest at a nearby hotel different from the rest of our group. Sleep eludes us. I soon realize that if our tickets turned out to be standby, then our other travelers on Iceland Air may also have the same problem. As I begin to close my weary eyes, I think about our travelers whose tickets are likely to also be standby. How in heaven's name can we rectify this unfolding chaos? Sleep is not in the cards, so early the next morning, Jim and I head back to the airport.

Throughout this unfolding drama, we have an ally organizing our pre-cruise schedules in Copenhagen. His name is Alex, and at every step along the way, we have contacted him with news of our travel nightmare. He makes certain that our travelers who fly into Copenhagen are met at the airport and escorted to their hotel. What a relief. So far, the travelers coming from other parts of the country have landed safely, and we know our five departing cruisers are well on their way to Denmark.

It is now Friday morning, and not only do we have to get our travelers to Copenhagen by Saturday morning, but we have to board that ship to sail with them. If there is such a thing as a travel nightmare, then we are living it.

Our taxi takes us back to the airport, where our fervent hope is that Iceland Air actually has seats for my understanding passengers. We arrive at the Iceland Air desk before it opens. As soon as the agent arrives, we pounce. A very helpful gentleman relays the news we had feared. The fifteen tickets are indeed just standby. By this time, we are masters at begging. The agent assures us that he will do everything in his power to find seats for all fifteen. My hopes are beginning to dwindle. Jim now comforts me, saying that, one way or another, we make the impossible possible.

A new set of plans are in the works. Jim will go back to Delta Airlines and try to implement plan B, C, D, and E to see if there are, by chance, any seats on flights into Denmark. Surely, we can make this work.

I am charged with boarding a bus to the hotel where the group is staying. Once there, I round up all my anxious cruise-goers in the lobby. I explain the situation and herd them back to JFK Airport. It is now ten A.M. The murmurings from the group are understandable. They are filled with worry. I completely understand, and I promise them that we will not rest until we get them all safely on flights. Once back at the Iceland Air desk, I speak with the agent. He works feverishly to accommodate us. This would be a great time for miracle number two.

While I hover over the Iceland Air agent, Jim is a stalwart presence at the Delta desk. He works with the management crew, diligently attempting to secure seats on another Delta flight. Tension is mounting as the hours tick by, and our high hopes are fading. I have only secured space on the Iceland Air flight for five of my travelers. It is now early afternoon. If we do not get these passengers on flights soon, they will not make it to the cruise in time. I am beginning to lose hope when, all of a sudden, I receive a call from Jim. He has one question: "Would anyone be willing to fly through Moscow and then on to Copenhagen?" So, I posed the question. Unbelievably, everyone answers a resounding "Yes!"

One by one, I call our travelers to meet Jim at the Delta desk to board the flight that takes them through Moscow. Eventually, all but five are confirmed to fly through Moscow where they will join Aeroflot Air to Copenhagen. To say I am nervous would be the understatement of the century. It is akin to sending your children off to kindergarten the first day. How will they be treated at the Moscow airport? What if they do not make their connecting flight? I have to put those thoughts out of my mind for now and concentrate on the five remaining travelers.

Iceland Air works carefully to make room for my anxious friends. Against all odds, they are confirmed on the flight. What a relief. My Iceland Air agent calmly walks my passengers onto the awaiting aircraft. All our "little birds" have literally flown the coop. It is time to declare this miracle number three.

Now, it is our turn to finally board another Air France flight bound for Paris and Copenhagen. Could this be true? It is now about four on Friday afternoon. I know the cruise departs the next day at three p.m. I wonder if we all are going to land in time on Saturday. As exhausted as I am, hope fills the air. For a few minutes, I am lulled into thinking positive thoughts. We are finally seated in the last two remaining seats on the plane. As we taxi down the runway, we come to an abrupt stop. There we sit for forty-five minutes waiting before we finally take off. I rightly determine that if we are delayed, so are our friends on the flight going through Moscow. If they miss their connecting plane, what will become of them? They do not have visas to travel through Russia. Will they be held at the airport, unable to leave? These thoughts reverberate in my mind and, as the hours pass, the more agitated I become. No sleep for night number two.

Charles de Gaulle airport in Paris never looked so good. We arrive early Saturday morning with plenty of time to board the remaining flight of our journey. By this point, we are on autopilot. As if in a complete daze, we find our seats and try to relax, praying that all would be well. With a group of our travelers somewhere in Moscow, fear and dread make my rapid heartbeat jump into overdrive! Fortunately, this leg of the journey goes smoothly, and by nine o'clock that morning, we walk into the Copenhagen airport. We are warmly greeted by Alex. I have never been so happy to see anyone in my life. He gives us big hugs and reassures us that most of our travelers have arrived safely. They are resting at the hotel. What terrific news! "What about the Moscow crew?" I ask. That flight is due in at half past eleven, but Alex is unable to verify if the rest of our travelers have made it safely onto the plane. I really do not know if it's worry or exhaustion beginning to overtake me.

I study the clock every few minutes and become convinced that our intrepid travelers are held in limbo inside an alien airport. As my worry turns to fear, Alex interrupts my thoughts. He tells me that several of our people already in Copenhagen have not received their luggage. He is going to hunt down the runaway bags. That he does. He manages to crawl over hundreds of pieces of luggage in the bowels of unclaimed luggage until he finds the lost bounty. Proudly, he emerges, victoriously holding all the missing bags. Maybe we are in for another miracle.

The clock ticks slowly until half past eleven. I check the incoming flight notices and remark that the flight from Moscow has indeed landed. I nervously stand at the waiting area, but there is no sign of any familiar passengers walking towards the terminal. It seems like an hour before the first stragglers begin to emerge. Still no sign of any of our folks. All of a sudden, Jim exclaims, "I see their luggage! I see their luggage!" Could this be true? Could this never-ending nightmare soon be over?

It is now noon, and we are just a couple of hours away from the ship's departure. Minutes are ticking away, and the fear still has not left me when, all of a sudden, I see our first traveler slowly come into view. The rest soon follow, and I greet them with shouts of joy and never-ending hugs. Biggest miracle of all! They regale me with the unbelievable story of how they were greeted in Moscow by Aeroflot officials and quickly whisked to their final flight. On board, they were treated royally.

Alex gathers us all—with all luggage present and accounted for—into the waiting van as we speed through Copenhagen. Before long, a very large cruise ship slowly comes into view. It is now a little after two in the afternoon, and the ship is due to pull up the gangplank and set sail at three. We are all thankful beyond belief that everything we have been through is over. We drag ourselves on board and give thanks for being there. Never have I been more relieved that a travel catastrophe has been averted. I do believe in miracles, and this journey is the manifestation of just that.

7

Oh Canada

Autumn is always a wonderful time to escort a group of travelers on a motor coach trip to beautiful Canada. The weather is a welcome relief to our hot summer days, and the scenery is beyond compare. On top of that, Canadians are kind and welcoming (hold on to that thought).

Believe it or not, this swing through Canada takes place just a week after the tragedy of 9/11. This presents many logistical challenges, but being a super tour guide, I attempt to overcome most obstacles in my path. The events of the past week seem like a completely different situation. The country is shell-shocked. The most unbelievable tragedy has occurred, and we are all in mourning. Not only for the lives lost, but also for the idea that we, as Americans, are immune from such an incredibly heinous act. I am in complete emotional turmoil. How can I think about travelling with a group, let alone entering a foreign country? The only thing to do is consult with my travelers. These are folks who all know each other. They belong to the same organization, so they can decide as a group the best way to proceed. Does the group even want to make this week-long journey north to Canada? Of course, there is the little matter of many dollars already paid in hotels and restaurants. This is truly a conundrum. Should we stay, or should we go? I understand their hesitation but also their mindset that perhaps a getaway will be "food for the soul." After much deliberation, the group chooses to move forward with our plans. Decision made; Canada, here we come!

I am traveling with the "fun bunch." These folks have known each other for years, and whenever they are on the coach, it is guaranteed that a good time will be had by all. Their nervousness at leaving during such a time of upheaval is tempered by the anticipation of a new adventure. On the day of departure, we are off to a great start. The group is a bit subdued, but nonetheless, anticipation is high. Wonderful sights like Niagara Falls, Montreal, and Quebec beckon.

During this particular time, I still need to bring enough cash and travelers checks to take care of our many expenses. So, I dutifully collect Canadian dollars and have my traveler's checks at the ready.

As we roll along, the mood of the travelers brightens. Even though the sense of the country is somber, we manage to enjoy one another's company, and at each stop, the local folks seem friendlier than usual. Even as we cross the Canadian border, the police there offer their thoughts and prayers. We feel encouraged as we visit Niagara Falls. Not only are the falls a majestic sight to behold, but we spy American flags everywhere, and we are buoyed by the good wishes.

Next stop: Montreal. A long drive means we arrive after dark. Our hotel is not a familiar one, but we are only here for a brief period, so not to worry. As usual, I step off the coach first with my purse in hand and stop at the reception desk. Standing there, I have a most uneasy feeling. The hotel does not seem up to my standards and the whole place seems sketchy. A few strangers are lurking around, and they seem to be eyeing the luggage that my driver has off-loaded from the coach. My eyes are definitely averted from the clerk behind the desk. As I present my ID to the desk clerk, I turn to see a "helper" fumbling with the guest list and room numbers. For some unknown reason, he seems befuddled by the process of tagging each piece with the correct room number. I am just about out of patience as I walk over to the bell hop and try to tackle this problem. After completing the task, I turn my attention back to the desk clerk. Uh oh! My purse is missing! It is nowhere in sight, and literally my life is in that purse. All my money, my ID, my passport, my credit cards are gone. I am now feeling a sense of panic unlike anything I have felt before. Of course, no one on the trip is aware of what just happened. I try not to panic. This is not easy when realizing the full weight of ramifications of such an event. This will greatly affect the tour. First step, get the passengers off the coach and get them to their rooms. Make certain they get their luggage, and try not to become hysterical. Quickly, I call my husband so he can stop the credit cards. Of course, the hotel personnel are unhelpful, which make things worse. I still have nearly an entire week of this trip left, and I do not have a single penny to my name or any identification. What am I going to do?

Number one, no one on the trip is to know what has happened. I need to keep things calm and drama-free. So, late that night, I make the decision to walk up to the local police station to tearfully file a report. The report reads as follows: "purse stolen, wallet stolen, passport gone, money gone, credit cards gone, traveler's checks gone, and driver's license gone." I stare at the report feeling completely defeated. I stumble back to the hotel filled with dread. How can I overcome the events of tonight?

There is no sleep for me. As I try to figure out a plan, Jim calls, and together, we will get through this calamity one day at a time. He will send a visa cash advance in the morning. Then, I open my suitcase. I realize that I still have some more American Express traveler's checks I know I can cash these in the morning. My tears fade at the thought of a way to get through tomorrow.

Morning dawns brightly, and my worry seems overwhelming. I still have no identification, and in the immediate aftermath of 9/11, I cannot imagine a way to manage this situation. How will I ever navigate the complexities of group travel with no personal identification or money in my pocket? Thoughts of sheer panic reverberate through my body. How can I stay calm in the face of all these challenges? Where is a little miracle when I need one? I must meet my group in the lobby promptly at nine in the morning. They all gather, blissfully unaware of the events of last night. The group is ready for a tour of the beautiful city of Montreal. I encourage them and try to keep the mood light. Soon, my guide appears. As he approaches me, I can see he has brought another guide with him. Wow! What luck? I quickly pull the main guide aside and relate my tale of woe. He decides that guide number two can stay with the group while he and I set about recovering enough funds to make it through to the next day. With his help, I collect the cash advance Jim has sent to the Western Union office. Quickly, we make our way to the American Express office where I am able to recoup the money from the stolen traveler's checks. Money in my pocket. What a relief. The Montreal tour guide is literally a godsend, no doubt about it. Without him, I would be dead in the water. Since I am unfamiliar with the labyrinth of twisted streets and many French signs, his guidance is invaluable. I know I could never complete this task without him.

After my mission of mercy, I rejoin the group and accompany them for a predetermined group lunch. Will my shaky hands or vacant stare give me away? Will anyone guess that something is seriously wrong? The only thing I can do is pretend that all is well. After greeting the group warmly, I hear stories of the great sights of this historic city. They are intrigued by this French-Canadian city. If only I could have been with them, but real life intervened. I now have the matter of how to pay for a delicious lunch for thirty people. My stomach is in knots as I share the news of my stolen purse with the restaurant manager. His response is a complete surprise. He is shocked by my predicament and apologizes on behalf of all Montreal. The manager further states that I can pay him when I return home. What a hopeful and encouraging response. Somehow, I know that indeed I can make it through the rest of the trip. That gentleman buoyed my confidence, and for the first time since I arrived in Montreal, I feel a sense of relief overtake me.

A few minutes later, I receive a call from my husband. He relates the good news that I am able to use my son's credit card for all future bills in Canada. That really cements my optimism. I will make it. Nothing will stop me now! Prayers of thanks seem so small in comparison to the bounty I just received. Now, I can confidently look my passengers in the eye with hope for the days ahead. No one ever has to know about "the case of the disappearing purse."

Things are looking up. I can actually pay the other hotel and restaurant bills. It is a great sense of relief much akin to driving out of a terrific thunderstorm into the bright sunshine. I can see the future, and it looks good.

We still have several days before we head for home. It is then that I realize I do not have a passport. I will never be able to cross the border back into the United States without it. Silently, severe panic sets in. I can just picture a coach full of people crossing safely back to America while I am hand cuffed and taken to a

Canadian jail. *Who will come to my defense? Who will post my bail?* These thoughts are swirling through my head like a rushing tide overtaking me. With shaking hands, I make a call to Jim. "What am I going to do?" I ask. To my utter relief, he tells me has already delivered an old passport of mine to the local passport office. They, in turn, sent a photocopy to the border crossing. *Would that be enough for me to safely reenter the United States? I have no idea if they will accept an old, faded passport photo.* Of course, thoughts consume me for the remainder of our journey.

At last, the time has come to cross the border. We inch toward the border check point. I secretly wonder if I will be carted off in front of everyone. *Will the jig be up? Will my secret be out of the proverbial bag?* At the border crossing, a guard steps onto the coach. Does he detect me shaking in my seat? He looks me over very carefully as I whisper to him that he has a photo of my passport in his office. With a quick nod and a thumbs up sign, he gives me the all clear. Instead of cuffing me and taking me away, he has given me a tremendous gift. I am free to continue home. Yes. "There really is no place like home." It seems as if all the powers that be are aware of my predicament and seamlessly let us cross back into the United States.

Meanwhile, no one on our trip has any idea what has happened. Am I a good actress or what? Perhaps, this performance is worthy of the travel woes Oscar. Good acting and the ability to carry on despite the worst circumstances comes in very handy on this trip and proves invaluable many times in the future.

8

Tour Guide Gone Bad

Ah, yes! Another trip to Europe is fast approaching. Once again, a large group of faithful travelers are ready to follow my lead and explore new horizons. How lucky am I? I have many folks who have faith in me and my ability to design an itinerary, which encourages others to pack their bags and join us. On one such occasion, I have planned a European adventure that includes Switzerland, Austria, and southern Germany. Who doesn't love visiting historic castles and charming medieval towns and villages? It is postcard perfect. Natural beauty is in abundance, and our group tends to "ooh" and "ah" at every bend in the road. How could anything go wrong when all seems so right?

The culmination of this odyssey is seeing the *Oberammergau Passion Play* in that small hamlet in Bavaria. Every ten years, the townspeople recreate the drama of Holy Week. This is the period between Palm Sunday and Easter. They have been recreating this story for over five hundred years, so it is quite a sight to witness the unfolding saga in person!

Confessions of a Crazed Tour Guide

Believe it or not, this is a most popular destination! I always have many requests to join me on such a special adventure. Well, that settles it; Bavaria, Germany, here we come. It is always very difficult to secure enough tickets to this famous play on my own, so in this case, I decide to partner with a larger tour organization. They can easily acquire enough tickets. This can be very beneficial but also presents a few challenges. First, we become part of a larger group and make use of their tour guides. Oops! Now I must relinquish control of my group to the larger company's guide. In the past, this has not presented any problems. The guides are always experts in their field and impart vast amounts of knowledge about the area we are visiting. The sheer amount of information is impressive, and I am filled with admiration. It makes me want to work that much harder to make certain I can perfect my proficiency.

As we embark on this new trip, life is good, and we are feeling relaxed. Of course, overseas flights are never easy, even in the best of circumstances. As usual, my merry band of aging travelers bring with them an odd assortment of ailments and worries about all that could possibly go wrong. Lots of nervous energy seems to buzz in the air like a swarm of bees. I too feel tingly and excited. The air hangs heavy in the summer heat, and I am thankful we are on our way to the cooler mountain air in Switzerland. Is there a more beautiful place on Earth? I think not. "The hills are alive with the Sound of Music!" Just the thought of this magical place conjures up images of breath-taking mountain views, Swiss men in lederhosen yodeling on the hillside, snow-capped hills, and crystal-clear mountain lakes.

When our plane lands in Zurich, we are met at the airport by our guide, Brett. I have an uneasy feeling about this young man. Usually, I am a pretty good judge of character. This fellow comes off as cocky and full of himself. *Hmm!* I think to myself; this is going to be an interesting trip experience. I know enough to withhold judgement until I see unprofessional behavior. Oh well, maybe I am just tired from a long flight and ready for a good nap.

Away we go. The group is off to our hotel for a well-deserved rest. As the dawn breaks the next morning, we are all excited and ready for a memorable day of viewing spectacular scenery. The sky is clear, and hopes are high. Brett joins the group, and we are on our way. Usually, our guides are founts of endless knowledge. Brett seems a little inadequate on the information front. Long periods of silence are interspersed with him reading from his notes. A big no-no for tour guides. We are supposed to have stories and current information committed to memory. Will my group realize that good old Brett is something short of stellar? Hopefully, they are more captivated by the majestic mountain scenery.

My nervousness is tempered by the group's delight. *June, stop worrying. We are having a terrific time.*

I am energized by the anticipation of our arrival in lovely Oberammergau, Germany. Can't wait for our group to savor the sights, walk the quaint streets, and take in the romantic atmosphere. It is a lovely historic town, one that dates back to the twelfth century. Many of the buildings are painted with murals reminiscent of fabled tales of old. It is a feast for the senses, and I encourage all to see as much as they can.

Everyone is giddy with anticipation. The Passion Play portrays the final week of Jesus' life in a most dramatic way. Townspeople are the actors, and in many cases, various roles are passed down through the generations. As the play unfolds, each day of Holy Week is a different act. Each part of this theatrical retelling of the final events of Jesus' life is filled with dramatic acting, music worthy of a famous opera, and opulent costumes. It is a sight to behold.

In addition, the stage is exposed to the elements, so the actors must deal with that added stress. All senses are heightened, and we are ready to be part of the experience.

Finally, we have taken in the sights of the town, and the main event is at hand. Brett walks us into the theater and disappears into the crowd. Oh well, he promises that he will meet us after the play has ended. We are to gather at the shuttle bus close to the theater.

Oh my! The pageantry, the drama, and the staging make this retelling of Holy Week really come to life. All my travelers are awed by the experience. This production has lasted several hours, and it is now dark as Jim and I gather our group. Mind you, hundreds of theatergoers are cascading out of the exits onto the street.

How will I ever corral my thirty slightly confused travelers and lead them to the waiting shuttle bus? Brett said he would meet us there, and I am counting on that! Jim and I are frantic as we gather our group. It is more akin to herding cats; as soon as one appears, another one wanders off. Little by little, we shepherd our flock and head for Brett and the meeting place.

I am equipped with a handy light that leads my group to the awaiting shuttle. As we near the appointed spot, Brett is nowhere in sight. Oh, this cannot be! He is our leader, and most of all, he knows where our bus is parked. After a few minutes, we make an executive decision. We will take our group on board the shuttle and hope we can determine where our bus is located. Now, my nervousness has reached fever pitch as we look for the appropriate lot. Only a faint memory of a lot number sticks in my head. We will have to go on faith and hope for the best. Well, my motto is "never let them see you sweat," but right now all bets are off! Our fearless leader has disappeared, and I only have a vague notion of where our coach can be found. Now may be a good time to mention that it is past ten o'clock at night. Our hotel is out of town, and the next morning is an early one for us all.

Like a hound dog on the scent of its prey, I surmise which lot contains our awaiting coach. Jim and I usher our passengers off the shuttle and prayerfully walk in the direction of our bus. We do not think any of our folks yet realize we are missing dear Brett. Eureka! There it is—a sight for sore eyes—our bus. Prayers of thanks are said as we help our flock onto the coach. Yes, all present and accounted for—except for one. I am fuming as I get off the bus and walk through the parking lot to look for you-know-who. As I search in the dark, all of the sudden a weaving figure comes towards me. Why, it is Brett, and he is as drunk as a skunk. Furious does not even begin to describe my feelings. "Where have you been?" I ask. Of course, I know the answer. He was sitting in the local beer hall getting hammered. My instructions to him are quite simple: "Do not say a word to the group!" I declare. "I will do all the talking."

Needless to say, it is a quiet ride back to the hotel. My group of weary travelers soak up the local culture and experienced a memorable evening! We do as well. Just different memories are made. Such is the life of a tour guide. Surprises at every turn!

9

Surprise Visitors

"Twas two days before Christmas, and all through the bus, not a senior was stirring, not even us." Once again, it is that perfect time of the year. Even aging seniors seem energized by the sights and sounds of the upcoming holidays. We are returning home after an invigorating day of shopping at a nearby outlet center. Each of my eager travelers is abuzz with tales of family plans and finding the perfect gift on our shopping trip. They are singing along with the carols sweetly wafting through the sound system. All seems right with the world. What could make the mood any brighter?

All of a sudden, the quiet conversation comes to a halt. Did I hear the pitter patter of tiny hooves on the roof of the coach? Did everyone hear it? Could it possibly be? From the far back of the bus I can spy a jolly old elf that "laughed when I saw him in spite of myself."

"Ho, ho, ho! Merry Christmas." Why, it is Santa himself. He has landed his sleigh on top of the coach, and he is anxious to spread joy to one and all. That bright red suit, white beard, and jaunty hat leave no doubt. He has come to magically turn a coach full of aging travelers into excited youngsters ready to reclaim a wonderful memory of their youth. As Santa slowly makes his way up the center aisle, he has one question for each. "Have you been good this year?" He claims to have a bag of coal for the naughty ones and sweets for those who say they have been good. I seem to be witnessing a minor miracle. Before me, one by one, each person's demeanor has changed. Faces are brighter. The smile on each face tells the tale. For a brief moment, the transformation is evident. Santa brings his magic that transforms us into believers.

"Santa, I have been very bad," says one. Hearty laughs fill the air, and Santa reaches into the naughty bag. Out comes a lump of coal that looks suspiciously like misshapen chocolate. One by one, each traveler declares their promise to be better in the coming year. Everyone is rewarded with a special treat. Laughter fills the rows, and the joyous sounds helps me realize we are all children at heart.

Now, Santa has visited with each traveler and his bag of tricks is empty. As he walks to the back of the coach, I hear him exclaim "Merry Christmas to all, and to all a good night." In the blink of an eye, he is gone. I thought I heard a top vent on the coach open. Could it be Santa springing onto the roof and into his sleigh? The faint reverberation of tiny hooves is the last impression of a magical event making Christmas dreams come true.

June Harvey

Through the years, many "surprise" visitors have been our special guests. None more famous than an interloper in Hartford, Connecticut. Another year, another sojourn north to New England. I am buoyed by the plethora of awesome destinations in this part of the country.

On this day, we are visiting the capital of this New England state. We are touring the state house in Hartford, Connecticut and then seeing the home of Mark Twain. It is a beautiful, Victorian structure filled with furnishings and mementos of that great writer. Even though he hailed from Hannibal, Missouri, Mark Twain settled here in the latter part of the nineteenth century. It is in this town that he raised his family and wrote many of his most famous books. What an honor to walk in the foot-steps of our iconic American author. He captured life in America so poignantly. It is no wonder that he is revered to this day. For many of us, the highlight is entering his study. Before us is his favorite desk and chair. I imagine the many days Mark Twain spent sitting there writing *Huckleberry Finn*, *The Adventures of Tom Sawyer*, and *A Connecticut Yankee in King Arthur's Court*. It is almost hallowed ground.

We are all awed by this experience and cannot imagine how the day could get any better. A lunch break is in order, and after an hour, we are to gather on the bus for our afternoon's activity. Each one files back onto the coach, and the mood is bright. It is almost as if no one wants to leave this historic home. As the driver begins to start the engine, I hear a faint knock on the door. Travelers whisper among themselves, wondering if there is a problem. The front bus door squeaks open, and to everyone's amazement, an almost mythical figure stands before them. The group looks in awe. He has bushy white hair and a prominent mustache. His suit is pure white, punctuated by a thin black tie knotted into a bow. His voice has a distinct southern drawl, and his physical presence quiets everyone. It is the man himself: Mark Twain. He is paying us a most extraordinary visit. His demeanor is unmistakable. There before us stands the embodiment of Samuel Clemmons. During the next two hours, he regales us with many tales of his life and writings.

Mark Twain seems to radiate sunlight. Dressed in white, he has a most unmistakable aura. Everyone sits in stunned silence as he begins to speak. His welcome is warm and inviting. He thanks us for visiting his home and then states that he would like to take us on a journey through time. Even if we cannot meet his friends in person, we hear from the man himself about memories of his neighbor, Harriett Beecher Stowe. Yes, he shares, they were great friends. He so admired her writings, especially *Uncle*

Tom's Cabin. Together, they shared a passion for racial equality. There is a bit of sadness in his voice as he recalls her passing.

Our coach rolls down the road as Mark Twain shares major points of interest. He tells us about the Old State House that dates from 1796. What a remarkable piece of history. Slowly, we come to a commemorative plaque that honors the Freedom Trail. It ran right through Hartford, and he tells us of meeting many residents who helped escaped slaves gain their freedom. Before long, our bus stops in front of the entrance to Cedar Hill Cemetery. It is here he relates that many of his friends are buried. First among them is Thomas Gallaudet, who founded a famous college for the hearing impaired. Many colleagues fought in the Civil War like Henry Ward Camp and John Burnham. We sit in rapt attention, knowing we are capturing a part of our history.

Mark Twain tells us the story of how one of his most famous books came about. It seems his childhood friend, Tom Blankenship, became the basis for the character Huckleberry Finn. Tom lived in a ramshackle house by the old mill in Hannibal. His escapades became legend. Mark Twain knew that Tom had to be the title character of his book. We are all captivated by this man, and we certainly do not want the afternoon to end. Before long, the bus comes to a stop. Our special guest bids us farewell and walks away into the evening mist. Each traveler is filled with awe. The experience seems a bit otherworldly. How did we manage to meet Mark Twain? Just a bit of luck, a time traveling bus, and being in the right place at the right time.

Confessions of a Crazed Tour Guide

Historic travel is a hallmark of mine. I am thankful to live in Virginia. We are surrounded by history on a daily basis, and my favorite destinations revolve around a memorable location or person. On this day, our group will visit both. It is a three hour drive from Southeastern Virginia to Charlottesville where we will visit the home of our third president, Thomas Jefferson. Jefferson designed and built his home, Monticello. Now, I am thoroughly familiar with the man. He was a pure Renaissance man. He was a writer, agronomist, inventor, and of course, a politician. I cannot wait to share the many aspects of this person with my group of travelers.

One by one, each person seems very eager for the events of the day to unfold. I am peppered with questions about his home and gardens. Will we receive a tour? Can we walk the grounds? How can we learn more about this important figure?

So many questions, so little time. Just relating important information can be dull, dry as a bone. My goal is to keep everyone engaged, and surprises along the way do just that. Creating memories, I like to say. On this particular day, I have enlisted the help of my husband, Jim. I have written a little play that hopefully will entertain the group and impart some helpful information about Mr. Jefferson, as he liked to be called.

Preparation is key to any successful trip. My play involves the narrator (me) and Jim dressed as Thomas Jefferson. He wears a tri cornered hat and a black cape. Since Jefferson was a prolific writer, he will hold a note pad and pen. At least he will look the part.

If I do say so myself, this little skit has turned out pretty well. All the information is there for Jim to commit to memory. I will give him cheat notes just in case he forgets a line or two, but I am certain he will not need them. About an hour from our destination, Jim quietly heads to the rear of the coach. He enters the rest room where he will magically transform himself into our third president.

I busy myself chatting with each traveler until I spy a fancy figure appear. Quickly, I move to the microphone and announce the arrival of a very special visitor. "Good sir," I say. "Who are you, and why are you here with us today?"

"Good day to you all," we hear. "I am Thomas Jefferson, and I am going to take you on a tour of my home." The crowd cheers at this statement and smiles abound. Things are going well, so I press on.

"Tell me, Mr. Jefferson how long did you live at Monticello?"

Now, my "actor" has a reassuring look on his face. "Why, I resided here at my mountain retreat for over twenty years. I designed my home at Monticello while I served as President."

This is proceeding very well. I think to myself so I ask another question. "What would you say is your greatest accomplishment?" I inquire.

"Thomas Jefferson" has a serious expression as he contemplates such a weighty answer.

Before long I hear, "Writing the Declaration of Independence."

Good answer, I think to myself. Now, we have everyone's attention, and I can tell Jim is really getting into his character. Boldly, I ask what year he made the Louisiana Purchase?

Now, I am expecting my reincarnation of Jefferson to answer such a simple question. Instead, I hear a lot of paper shuffling and a look of bafflement. Uh oh! Things are not proceeding as I had hoped. My husband has lost his place and from the look on his face I can tell he cannot remember a single thing about the rest of the play. He starts to ad-lib.

Instead of the group wondering what is going on with their onboard visitor, they start laughing in unison. The more questions I ask and the more answers I correct, the louder the laughter. Evidently, messing up is a lot more entertaining than Jim playing the straight man. The rest of the skit is a comedy of ad-lib errors. Roars of cheers for our man of the hour reverberate throughout the coach. Folks love this revival of Thomas Jefferson. Once we arrive at Monticello, a proper guide will invite us into the world of Mr. Jefferson. Until then, we are content to see the humor in Jim's portrayal of the man. He receives hearty congratulations on a job well done.

New York

10

New York, New York's a Wonderful Town

I literally have New York City running through my veins! Believe it or not, it is my hometown. Just one of the eight million stories in the naked city, I like to say.

One of my favorite trips each year is the annual trek to the Big Apple. I take holiday travelers there each year just before Christmas. Trust me, that is when New Yorkers are on their best behavior!

Each trip consists of the requisite visit to Radio City to see the Rockettes and the Christmas Spectacular. Touring the various neighborhoods is always on the agenda, and Chinatown is a fan favorite. My tour guide friend, Dennis, and I would put our heads together and formulate ideas for a tour that highlights the hidden treasures of the many small, quaint neighborhoods. Around every corner of Lower Manhattan, there is a unique story to tell. After all, these neighborhoods were originally settled by immigrants.

Confessions of a Crazed Tour Guide

As each hopeful transplant arrived at Ellis Island, they made a beeline for their relatives who preceded them. Thus, the many neighborhoods that dot this part of Manhattan are replete with authentic sights, smells, and tastes of those immigrants who added to the rich history of New York. Dennis has many unique perspectives that bring the history of this great city to life.

One of the great neighborhoods in the world is Chinatown. I can close my eyes and conjure up Mott Street, the epicenter of the nation's largest Chinatown. It is a narrow lane, but it is bustling and alive with people talking rapidly in Cantonese. Many colorful overhead signs announce each shop and restaurant. Shopkeepers stand outside and beckon shoppers to come inside. The scents are alluring! The smell of fried egg rolls is hard to resist, and the sight of ducks hanging in a shop window has me averting my eyes! It is a cacophony of the senses, and I feel alive and exhilarated just by being there

On one particular tour of Chinatown, Dennis regales us with his usual stories of the unique nature of the Big Apple. We are with a group of my travelers who are ready for a fun experience, one that will provide memories that linger long after we return home. Ah, the excitement builds! As we get closer to our destination, the sights come alive. People are walking briskly down Canal Street (the main thoroughfare), street vendors are hawking their wares, and we can almost smell the local cuisine. As the coach stops, Dennis ushers us off the bus, and we are encouraged to visit some of the local shops while he does his own shopping.

Yes, he will gather a variety of tasty treats and then meet back up with the group to sample the authentic cuisine of Chinatown.

That brings to mind my own top-secret mission. I am accompanied by two of my good friends. They are intent on securing a most prized possession. So, we begin our quest, like big game hunters on the prowl for their prey. We begin our hunt for a most rare artifact. This unique object is prized by many, yet owned by just a few. How could we secure such a gem? This object could only be found in the back rooms of small shops deep within the bowels of Mott Street. I alone know this secret, and it is up to me to bring two friends along for this epic hunt. We have to act fast or go home empty-handed. As we walk down a side street, I spy the perfect shop. Small, but long and deep. Only the most ardent shoppers here know that the good stuff is well concealed behind closed doors in one such shop. As we enter the store, I ask the proprietor if she indeed had any special Prada handbags in her fine establishment.

As if on a secret mission as undercover agents, the owner says in hushed tones, "You come with me; you come with me." As she says this, her finger is over her lips as if to underscore the secrecy of the mission.

Like lambs to the slaughter, we follow her to the back of the shop. Before you know it, she opens a door to a broom closet and ushers us to go in. It suddenly dawns on me that this might not be the safest move I have ever made. Were we soon to be kidnapped and ushered into a dark tunnel that leads to a ship in the Hudson?

What if our families never see us again? Thoughts are swirling through my head as we all step inside the closet. All of a sudden, the door slams behind us! *What is going on?* I wonder.

Now the shop owner stands before us in this dimly lit closet and starts handing out many of her not-so-official high-end purses. They are coming at us so fast we literally have to bat these flying projectiles away before they hit us in the face. This lady is so eager to sell us her illicit contraband that she can't control herself.

"You like this one? You like this one?" is her repeated plea.

The onslaught of "fake" purses is coming at us fast and furious. It is hard to think coherently. Our intention is to snag the most prized possession. We had come with one thought in mind. Prada or bust! Quickly, we return to our senses because time is running out, and if we hesitate, we will come away from our quest empty-handed. *June, snap to, and make a decision.*

We all know that Prada is the epitome of high design. With a purse like that on my arm, folks would be very impressed.

Now, the decision time has come. We must be victorious and secure our intended prey. Of course, one of the staples of Chinatown is bargaining. The shopkeeper wants a cool fifty dollars for each purse. Is she kidding? What kind of offer is that? I must use my bargaining skills to secure our prizes. This is my forte. Never pay retail is my golden rule.

"No, that is too much," I bravely state. I offer a more affordable thirty-five dollars, and the requisite bargaining ensues. Finally, we agree on the price. I am overjoyed. It is a hard-fought battle, but victory is at hand. We settle on our basement bargain price and revel in our good fortune. Now, everyone will be envious of our knockoff purse prowess. Before we leave the shop, the owner stuffs each purse into a black garbage bag tied at the top. "You tell no one; you tell no one!" is her parting comment. We swear our secrecy and scurry swiftly away, laughing at our adventure and good fortune.

Just another tale in the naked city . . . until you hear sirens everywhere.

Even time in a suspicious clothes closet in Chinatown can't dampen my desire to find the ultimate bargain. No obstacle is too great. No trepidation is too severe to keep me from finding the ultimate prize. I am energized by the constant hum of traffic, the hordes of folks on the city streets, and the constant visual bombardment of larger-than-life billboards and lights so bright that, even at midnight, onlookers may don sunglasses. Not this fearless tour guide. Why, my recent experience only heightens my desire to excavate the deepest, darkest recesses of Mott Street in Chinatown.

On another day, I am escorting a small group to Chinatown in Lower Manhattan. These travelers are experienced New York devotees. Each one is thoroughly familiar with the intricately woven quaint streets and alleyways that are a hallmark of this part of the city. Each one of us shares a desire to feel the excitement of a cacophony of sounds and the rich enticing aromas coming from the food vendors. Of course, snagging a bargain is an added benefit. My intrepid group is counting on me to find just the right shop that offers the best leather coats. Years of mingling with the shop owners helps me lead us in the direction of a bargain hunters dream. As we enter one of my favorite shops, a blaring sound pierces our senses. Loud sirens alert owners that the police want to close down any place selling counterfeit merchandise labelled as authentic. Faster than you can say Gucci, we are ushered out of this shop. My ladies are surprised by this turn of events and look bewildered. Oh no! Our quest is not yet realized. We could not go back to the hotel empty-handed, so hurriedly, we turn down a side street and are pleased to see a shop still open. Quietly, we stroll inside. Out of the blue, I spy a shopper haggling with the shopkeeper who asks, "Is this jacket real leather?"

The owner replies, "No. it's all fake!" Our ears perk up as the shopper once again inquiries about the quality of leather as she looks at a different jacket. The reply comes back quickly: "No, it is all fake, fake, fake." The shopper nervously runs out of the store. We each quickly pick out a leather garment and proceed to pepper the owner with similar questions. "Is this real leather?" Each reply is the same. Now, we are in the driver's seat. Like contestants on a scavenger hunt, we are buoyed by the nervous expression on the owner's face. She wants to make a sale and fast. We quickly realize the owner thinks we are undercover police. Now is the time to pounce. One by one, each of us secures a lovely "designer" original. We pay a greatly reduced price for each leather item as we are assured they are all fake. Quickly, we exit the shop reveling in our good fortune. This shopping safari netted us trophies worthy of the fanciest store on Fifth Avenue.

11

Christmas Dreams Come True

What could be better than a trip to New York City just before the holiday season? Oh, the array of lights, the myriad of decorations, and the glittering, larger-than-life Christmas tree at Rockefeller Center all put even the most Scrooge-like New Yorker in a more festive mood.

All the more reason to offer to take a group of cheery travelers to the Big Apple in December. As we leave on the "Christmas Bus Express," everyone is in a jolly mood. Filled with anticipation, my merry band of seniors can't help but burst into song. Sounds of "Jingle Bells" waft through the coach, and the anticipation is building as, at long last, the skyline of Manhattan comes into view.

I must admit, I get chills every time I see the skyline of the fabled city come into awesome sight. Every time I catch a glimpse of the Empire State Building and the 1776 Tower, I am reminded of a childhood spent exploring every inch of the city with great relish. Now, I get to share that knowledge with anxious visitors each December.

One of the things I do not look forward to is the never-ending congested streets, honking horns, and snail's pace movement. It takes longer for our coach to creep to our hotel than it did to make the long drive from Virginia. Not a moment too soon, our hotel comes into view. Now, my weary travelers can get a little rest and relaxation before we have to gather together and walk to Radio City Music Hall later this evening.

This year, I have two full buses and a hundred travelers who have come to take a bite out of the Big Apple. Yes, you heard me correctly. I now have to guide all these folks through the bustling city streets. Wow! How can I get all these folks safely from point A to point B? Fortunately, I am no stranger to *Star Wars* and Luke Skywalker's lightsaber. I figured if it was good enough for Luke, then may the force be with me as well.

Lucky for me, I am an ardent internet shopper, and I am able to locate multiple lightsabers in a variety of illuminated holiday colors. These long, gleaming, colorful beauties are a beacon in the night. With the help of relatives and volunteers, my seniors can follow the lights to Radio City. At the end of the performance, the same rainbow-colored lights are there to guide everyone back to the hotel. "Follow the light" is my constant refrain.

Luckily, this is a great success, and I am patting myself on the back for cleverly solving a vexing problem. Once home, I carefully put my sabers away, ready for another day.

Fast forward to Christmas morning. As always, we have our whole family at our home for fun and festivities. Our daughter, her husband, and our youngest grandchildren come in time for Christmas. Since our grandkids are young, Christmas morning is that much more wonderful. Our five-year-old grandson is a real *Star Wars* fan. He loves everything about that series, especially the hero, Luke Skywalker. His only wish from Santa is a Luke Skywalker lightsaber. That sounds reasonable. No problem.

Well, under the tree early that morning our sweet grandson spies a long, wrapped package with his name on it. As if on a frantic mission, he unwraps the glittery package. There, in all its glory, is a lightsaber. Overcome with joy, he states, "But I thought Luke Skywalker's lit up."

Our sweet five-year-old is holding a foamy saber with no light. Now, our boy looks quite disappointed, and my daughter looks at me. Her eyes seem to say, *What do we do now?*

Of course, being Super Grandma, I have the answer. Lucky for me, I have a treasure trove of lightsabers at my fingertips.

Quietly, I whisper to my daughter that the answer to her dilemma is in my bedroom. I tell her where to find the glowing answer to prayer. Quietly, she tiptoes upstairs, and in a few minutes, returns with the saber hidden behind her back. Stealthily, she hides it behind the tree and sits down again for more Christmas morning joy. Before long, our grandson makes his way around the back of the tree. We hear a giant squeal and a "Wow!"

"Santa brought me my light-up saber!!" He is overjoyed, and we all look at each other with obvious delight.

All is right with the world—or is it? Out of the mouth of a babe, we hear, "But I thought Luke's lightsaber was red!" Oh no, my daughter has brought down a green one. One more silent trip upstairs to my secret stash reveals the all-important shining, shimmering, glowing red sword, and down she comes once again with one more of our boy's special request. To everyone's sheer joy, the shouts of "Just what I always wanted!" reverberate through the house.

I have always known that tour guides are blessed with a sixth sense of predicting the unpredictable, but this is by far my greatest victory to date!!

Epilogue

Life is never dull! At least, not when you are a tour guide. I can honestly say that, in over twenty years of group travels, I encountered at least one surprise on each trip. From the early mornings of meeting my coaches to the varied groups of travelers, to the multitude of destinations, I came to expect the unexpected. What I could always count on was the one traveler who was usually late, thereby throwing off a perfectly timed schedule. Perhaps an unexpected traffic jam would set my nerves on edge. At that point, the dominoes would begin to fall. Frantically calling vendors along the route to warn of our late arrival would often be the order of the day. Being fast on my feet and quick to mobilize plan B helped to save the day many times, all the while making traveler's feels at ease. "Who, me? Worry?" On the outside, I projected calm assurance. Inwardly, I was a bundle of nerves and anxiety. The thing that kept me coming back time and again was the many travelers who became friends.

Seeing smiling faces early in the morning in turn filled me with joyful anticipation. Knowing I was able to brighten a senior's day was the big pay-off.

This book is replete with tales of the unexpected! From getting directions to the wrong hotel to having a sick traveler on an overseas adventure, to bailing an octogenarian out of jail, I was tested both mentally and physically. After each such encounter, I learned a little bit more about my internal fortitude. The thing that surprised me the most was that, in each case, I remained steadfast. I realized I was stronger than I thought. Each misadventure increased my self-confidence and drive. Do I wish some of the events had never happened? Of course I do, but then again, I would not have had stories I could share. Hopefully, these stories put a smile on your face, dear reader.

People always ask if I would do it all again. The answer is an emphatic *yes*. I compiled more adventures and misadventures than most people have in a lifetime. When I look back on my career as a tour guide, I usually have a big grin on my face and a chuckle in my voice. It has been a great career, and believe it or not, there are more stories left untold, so stay tuned!